Animals All Around

Do Bears Buzz?

A Book About Animal Sounds

Buzz? Buzz?

Buzz? Buzz?

Buzz?

Written by Michael Dahl
Illustrated by Sandra D'Antonio

Content Consultant: Kathleen E. Hunt, Ph.D.
Research Scientist and Lecturer, Zoology Department
University of Washington, Seattle, Washington

Reading Consultant: Susan Kesselring, M.A., Literacy Educator
Rosemount-Apple Valley-Eagan (Minnesota) School District

PICTURE WINDOW BOOKS
MINNEAPOLIS, MINNESOTA

Animals All Around series editor: Peggy Henrikson
Page production: The Design Lab
The illustrations in this book were rendered in marker.

Picture Window Books
5115 Excelsior Boulevard
Suite 232
Minneapolis, MN 55416
1-877-845-8392
www.picturewindowbooks.com

Printed in the United States of America.
1 2 3 4 5 6 08 07 06 05 04 03

Library of Congress Cataloging-in-Publication Data
Dahl, Michael.
Do bears buzz? / written by Michael Dahl ; illustrated by
Sandra D'Antonio.
p. cm. — (Animals all around)
Summary: Introduces a variety of sounds that are made
by animals.
ISBN 1-4048-0100-6 (lib. bdg.)
1. Animal sounds—Juvenile literature. [1. Animal sounds.]
I. D'Antonio, Sandra, 1956— ill. II. Title.
QL765 .D24 2003
591.59'4—dc21
2002155008

No! Bees buzz.

A bee's buzz is the sound of its busy, beating wings.
Bee wings beat so fast that you can hardly see them.
They beat about 190 times every second.

Do bears bark?

No! Dogs bark.

Dogs bark to let you know that they are lonely or hungry, or because they see or smell a stranger nearby. Dogs also bark when they get excited and want to play.

Do bears moo?

No! Cows moo.

Cows can moo while their mouths are full of tender, tasty grass. Cows moo to call their calves. They also moo to keep in touch with other cows as they move and munch their way through the meadow.

Do bears oink?

No! Pigs oink.

Pigs oink, squeal, grunt, snuffle, and snort.
Mother pigs oink when it's time for their piglets to eat.
Pigs use many different kinds of oinks to talk to each other.

Do bears cluck?

No! Chickens cluck.

Mother hens cluck softly to their babies even while the chicks are still inside their eggs. After the chicks hatch, they can find their mother by listening for her own special cluck.

12

Do bears honk?

No! Geese honk.

Geese honk as they flap and fly together across the sky. Honking helps the geese keep track of each other without having to turn their heads to look.

Do bears hiss?

No! Snakes hiss.

When some snakes are scared, they let out a startling hiss.
Before a snake hisses, it breathes in a large gulp of air.
The extra air helps the snake hiss loud and long.

Do bears meow?

No! Kittens meow.

Kittens meow when they want attention from their mother.
If they are hungry, the kittens open their tiny mouths and meow loudly.
When their mother feeds them, their meows turn to peaceful purring.

Do bears cry?

No! Loons cry.
A loon's cry sounds like a haunting call, or a weird, warbling wail. A female loon cries to attract males. A male loon cries to let other birds know that he claims the lake as his home.

Do bears growl?

Sounds That Animals Make

Some animals make soft sounds.

busy buzzes	bees
hisses and swishes	snakes
quiet clucks	chickens

Some animals make loud sounds.

cries and wails	loons
sharp barks	dogs
hungry meows	kittens

Some animals make low, deep sounds.

murmurs and moos	cows
grumbles and growls	bears

Some animals make rough sounds.

oinks and grunts	pigs
harsh honks	geese

23

Words to Know

grunt—a deep, short sound

meadow—a big, usually low area of land that is mostly covered with grass

snort—a short, rough sound made through the nose

snuffle—a deep, sniffing sound made through the nose

squeal—a sharp, high sound

warbling—going between high and low notes very fast when singing or crying out. Loons can make warbling cries.

Index

To Learn More

At the Library

Davis, Katie. *Who Hoots?* San Diego: Harcourt, 2002.

Fleming, Denise. *Barnyard Banter.* New York: Holt, 1994.

Leonard, Marcia. *Animal Talk.* New York: HarperFestival, 2000.

Phillips, Mildred. *And the Cow Said Moo!* New York: Greenwillow, 2000.

On the Web

Minnesota Zoo
http://www.mnzoo.com/index.asp
Explore the Minnesota Zoo online, including a Family Farm. See pictures of the animals and visit the Kids' Corner with animal puzzles, games, and coloring sheets.

Zoological Society of San Diego: e-zoo
http://www.sandiegozoo.org/virtualzoo/homepage.html
Visit this virtual zoo with a Kid Territory. The section for kids includes animal profiles, games, zoo crafts, and even animal-theme recipes, such as Warthog Waffles.

Want to learn more about the sounds that animals make? Visit FACT HOUND at *http://www.facthound.com.*